Secrets of a Six-Figure Expert

Build a Profitable, Fulfilling Business
By Positioning Yourself As
The Natural Expert In Your Field

I0473143

Rob Cuesta

The Six-Figure Business Mentor
For Coaches, Consultants and Trainers

First published in Great Britain by Solution Academy
Limited in 2012.

Solution Academy Limited
300 Rempstone Road
Merley
Wimborne
BH21 1SZ
United Kingdom

Copyright © 2012 by Robert Cuesta-Sevillano
ISBN 978-1-4716-3680-6

CONTENTS

INTRODUCTION

Hello. My name is Rob Cuesta, former accountant and corporate management consultant, now a successful business growth mentor and leadership expert.

In my first book, "More Clients, More Money, More Fun" I set out a simple plan for growing your business. It's a model that has been followed by many coaches, both in starting out and in growing an existing business.

But the more I thought about it, the more I came to realise that it wasn't what I had done myself. And it wasn't what the many six- and seven-figure coaches and consultants I know were doing in growing their businesses.

It was a simple observation by a participant in a $16,000 mentoring program that led directly to this book.

I was explaining the traditional sales funnel model, the ultimate expression of the principle of Ascension I set out in "More Clients, More Money, More Fun".

I was talking about getting clients to go through a series of value steps: free book or report, $27 CD, $97 DVD set, $247 workshop, etc. (you've undoubtedly seen the model in use, and have probably been through a few funnels over the years).

Suddenly, a hand shot up in the front row. "But that's not how you got us here!"

And I realised it was true. The 24 people in front of me had never bought a CD, or a DVD set, or a retreat, or anything else. They had signed up directly for a high-end mentoring program without the usual long, tedious, creeping distraction of the sales funnel.

That evening I realised that for years I'd been sidestepping questions about my own sales funnel. For the simple reason I'd never really needed one.

Even when I was running my NLP training school, 80% of the people who came on my £2,000 NLP practitioner training had never had any dealing with me before they walked in for the first day of the course. And the rest had been to a one-day introductory event.

My very successful six-figure corporate coaching and consulting business had no funnel either. I've built a global business, with clients like HSBC and ABN Amro. The world's largest professional service firm flies me to the US regularly to coach its partners around their personal brand. And I fly around the world training leaders in software giant Microsoft.

I have clients across the globe, from Vancouver to Beijing, and from Sydney to Stockholm.

Without a funnel.

But in the back of my mind I wondered whether what I had done was something unusual, that others wouldn't be able to replicate.

So I looked around at other coaches, consultants and trainers with six- and seven-figure and I saw that they were actually "breaking all the rules" too.

That was the moment the Six Figure Blueprint was born, and with it the idea of The Natural Expert.

You see it's quite simple. You know that you are great at what you do. In fact, you're an expert at it. More than that, even, you are the one person who does what you do the way that you do it. And for that reason, there is a group of potential clients out there for whom you are the one, the only, the *natural* choice in solving their challenges.

Your challenge is letting them know you're there.

That's what this book is about.

So alongside my thriving corporate business, I developed an equally important part of my professional life, mentoring coaches and consultants across the globe and helping them to grow their practice.

I do it for two main reasons.

First, because I enjoy it. But more importantly, because I don't want anyone else to go through the years of heartache and stress that came before my current success.

Like you, I went into practice on my own because I wanted to be independent. I wanted the freedom to choose, when I worked, where, and for whom. I wanted challenge, choice and above all to create a legacy.

I set up my business in 2002, leaving a successful career as a manager in Deloitte Consulting, one of the world's largest management consultancy firms. With that pedigree, and an MBA from a top European business school, I was certain that clients would flock to my door.

It took me three years to realise my mistake. Three years that took me to the verge of bankruptcy.

By January 2005 I was £106,000 in debt, and determined to turn things around. Less than 12 months later my fees were nearing six figures.

And things continued to improve until 2008, when the world changed and I realised that the business model I had built was not sustainable.

Unfortunately, it took a while for my lifestyle to catch up with reality. I was still living a six-figure lifestyle—flying first class, staying in 5-star hotels, wearing hand-made suits and driving a very fast, very red sports car—while only earning £25,000. I had to learn (VERY quickly) how to get my practice back on track.

I did it; along the way creating a business that is sustainable and fulfilling. In the last 10 years, I have

- Walked on hot coals (literally!)

- Created a £100K practice, lost it in the Credit Crunch, then rebuilt it in the middle of the worst recession in over 70 years

- Taught members of the armed forces the skills of extreme "persuasion" (ahem!)

- Climbed volcanoes in Iceland

- Walked across the Grand Canyon

- Watched the midnight sun from a naturally heated hot-tub in the snow in Iceland

- Lost my shirt in Vegas

- Changed my car from red, sporty and thirsty to something far more ecological

- And a lot else that was as much about fun and lifestyle as they were about business growth

To me, the secret of building a thriving, fulfilling practice is to live life on your own terms and have fun building your brand and your business.

And in this book I will share with you my most powerful secrets. I will show you how simple it actually is to grow a fulfilling AND profitable business, when you know where to focus your time, money and energy.

Underpinning everything is a simple philosophy based on building a community around you who love what you do and also how you do it, creating massive value for them, and positioning yourself in their eyes as the only person it makes sense to do work with.

Now, this book is deliberately brief. I wanted to give you something you could read during your commute, in a lunch break, or a quiet moment on the beach.

Because of that, I don't have space to share with you *everything* I know. Even if this book were 200 pages long, I would still only be scratching the surface of how to grow and develop a profitable professional practice. So where I can I will suggest how you can learn more, and at the end of the book I will tell you how you can join me to continue your journey towards becoming the natural expert in your field with a thriving six-figure practice.

A note on terminology

Throughout this book I will refer to something I call the "Professional Expert" industry: people who are paid to be experts in our field. We make our money by charging for our expertise, knowledge, ideas, experience, reflection, advice or even implementation—doing stuff with or on behalf of our clients.

It's an "industry" that includes fields as diverse as coaches, consultants, accountants, lawyers, financial advisers, trainers, architects, therapists and many others.

So for the sake of brevity (and because I'm not being paid by the word), I'll refer to Professional Experts and, as those professional experts build a stronger position in their field, Natural Experts.

For similar reasons, I will frequently use the masculine profiles "he" and "his". That's purely to avoid having to write "he or she" or the horrible "s/he", or referring to one person as "they"!

Rob Cuesta
The Six-Figure Business Mentor
www.RobCuesta.com

March 2012

THE JOURNEYMAN
AND THE GURU

When I graduated from university, my first real job was as an accountant in one of the "Big 4" firms (the name given to the largest accounting firms in the world).

Working in a small, provincial office of a major company gave me a unique insight into growing a professional practice. We were a major brand, but growing our business the same way as one- or two-person firms in the same town.

And the mainstay of our marketing was networking and brochures.

The Professional Expert industry has traditionally been built on two ways of getting clients. And I think BOTH of those models are broken.

The first is what I call the "Journeyman" model. In mediaeval England a "journeyman" was a craftsman who was just starting out on their career and wanted to become a member of a guild. So the guild told them "study hard, practice - for free if necessary - take our exams and one day you can be qualified (accredited, or certified, or chartered, or whatever the guild wanted to call it) THEN clients will hire you because we've told them you are worthy to be a member of the profession".

So the journeyman worked hard, practiced (often doing work for free just to get the experience), took their professional tests, and one day they got their professional certificate, complete with gold letters, a wax seal, and letters to put after their name.

But no clients came. So the newly qualified journeyman went back to the school that trained them to find out how to get clients. "Get some business cards, and put the letters after your name. Then get some brochures printed with our crest on. THEN clients will come."

So the journeyman got business cards, and brochures, and went to network breakfasts. And lunches. And conferences. They asked craftsmen in other trades if they would put their brochures and business cards on display in their shop.

And they did MORE free work, in the hope that people would be overcome with gratitude and hire them, or else send them more clients.

With little variation, it's the model still recommended by about 90% of professional training schools, whether you're training to be a coach, accountant or lawyer.

It's hard work. It's thankless. And very few manage to make a decent living from it. As I pointed out in my first book, "More Clients, More Money, More Fun", a survey by the International Coaching Federation found that coaches around the globe earn an average of just $50,000 (£30k). 79% of dentists feel they are working too hard and make too little for the amount of training they had to do. In the UK only one accounting firm in three reports annual turnover of more than £100,000, and a third make less than £50,000. And the average salary for a lawyer is £51,000.

I call it "the 50K wall", and I frequently get calls from professionals who have run into it at full speed. It hurts!

So what's the alternative? It's what I call the "Guru Model".

Here, you go out and find a niche - but one that's large "enough" - and gather a list of tens of thousands, or better yet hundreds of thousands of people who *might* be interested in what you do, then you start to feed them information, and every so often you give them a hurdle to pass (like buying something) so you can slowly whittle the list down to a few thousand who want to pay you money, and a few dozen who want to pay you SERIOUS money.

It's the Guru model, because the idea is to position yourself as the guardian of some deep dark secret reserved only for a hidden few. You hide yourself at the top of a metaphorical mountain and wait for the select few who are devoted enough to make it to the top.

The problem is, it used to work but it doesn't any more.

Getting thousands of people to sign up for your list is hard work, and the blighters keep unsubscribing. Even if you can get them on your list, and keep them there, there's no guarantee they'll open your emails.

Worse still, though, the guru model relies on selling information. Well information these days is pretty much free thanks to the internet, so why would people pay you for something they can find out for free?

Positioning yourself as The Natural Expert creates a business where you'll never have to go networking or cold call a prospect ever again. The Natural Expert Model positions you as being so clearly different from the other professional experts who claim to do what you're doing, that it makes no sense for your prospective clients to hire anyone but you.

In the next chapter we'll be addressing one of the biggest curses of the Professional Expert Industry: the sales funnel. I see more practitioners held back by this stumbling block than by any other: the sheer overwhelm, fear and procrastination at the thought of having to create a dozen products to sell to clients can stop a gifted expert in their tracks.

But that's about to change for you.

A LEAKY FUNNEL IS A SIEVE

For the last few years I've been toeing the party line, saying "go out, build a sales funnel, create lots of products at different price points, and get people to show how much they're willing to pay to work with you".

And I'm sorry, but that model just doesn't work anymore.

It's a tried and tested approach. One that came from the world of retail marketing, and one which--by and large--has worked well in the Professional Expert industry for many years.

But even mainstream marketers are leaving it behind.

In case you've been asleep or in jail for the last 20 years, let me recap.

The sales funnel model says that if you want someone to pay you £5,000 for your coaching programme first you need to see if they'll pay you £1,000. And to know that, you may need to see if they'll pay you £500, so first you'll need to sell them something for £100, which probably means you need to see if they'll buy at £10 first. Who do you sell that £10 product to? The tens of thousands of people who have downloaded your free product first.

So you need to create and sell 5 products before you can get people to pay you what you're actually worth.

That's a lot of work!

The second problem is that people don't buy all those products at the same time. Even if it took them a month to work through each product and be ready for the next, its six months before you get to see them. And the reality is it usually takes a lot longer. I've heard of people taking 3 years to get through someone's sales funnel.

The third problem is that it's not really a funnel as such. With a funnel, everything you pour in the top comes out of the bottom eventually.

The traditional sales funnel is actually more like a very leaky sieve: a lot of people fall out of holes along the sides, and only a few are left in the bottom to become your top-paying clients.

So what does that mean? Well, assume a fairly optimistic upsell rate of 10% for your products at each stage (in other words 1 in 10 people who buy a product in your funnel will buy the next one).

If you want just one client at £5,000, you'll need 10 people to buy your £1,000 product, which means 100 need to buy the £500 product, which means 1,000 buy the £100 product, which means you have to sell 10,000 of the £10 product, which means you need 100,000 in your mailing list FOR EACH HIGH END CLIENT YOU WANT TO HAVE.

Now, some steps will convert better than others: for example, if you put in a live workshop at some stage, and you've learned how to sell from the stage, you can get as much as 60% conversion or more. But that doesn't take away from the fact that you need to find a LOT of leads for this model to work.

And that's a huge problem in itself.

But for me, the killer is that it's just so "transactional": you see, people only stay in your funnel as long as they're buying from you. It's all about "qualifying people out" if they aren't buying. So the underlying assumption is that if someone doesn't buy then they are, from the point of view of this model, of no value to you.

That's a horrible way to look at it!

Being The Natural Expert is all about creating a community—I call it your tribe—where your audience grows all the time, and where there are no hoops to working with you, where your focus is on engaging, not selling, and where people want to spend £5,000, £10,000, £15,000 or even more with you very early on.

No more £27 CDs, as I promised!

OK, in the next chapter we'll look at one change that has happened in the world which has undermined the value of most of the work we do in the Professional Expert industry.

THE DEATH OF THE INFORMATION ECONOMY

I want to talk to you about one of the changes that has done more than anything else to devalue the work of Professional Experts.

You've probably heard it said many times that we live in "the Information Economy", and we need to become information marketers, selling Information Products.

Here's the thing though.

People think the internet created the information economy.

It didn't.

An industrial economy is one in which people pay for the outputs of industry. Whoever controls the most industrial resources "wins".

An agricultural economy is one based on the value of agricultural products. Whoever has access to the most agricultural resources "wins".

So in the information economy it would be information that had the greatest value, and victory would be assured by controlling access to information.

But in the age of Internet it's actually almost impossible to control the flow of information. If you have a piece of critical strategic information, it won't be long until your competitors get it too.

People were selling information in books and newspapers and audio programmes and video programmes long before the Internet came on the scene.

The Information Economy relied on scarcity to keep prices high. Put simply, access to information was controlled by a few big publishing and media companies, and if you wanted that information you had to pay for it.

Then along comes the Internet, and suddenly everyone has access to information on demand, and the ability to publish their own information at will, all at zero/minimal cost. The value of information became zero overnight.

In other words...

THE INTERNET KILLED
THE INFORMATION ECONOMY

People don't want to pay for information any more.

You'd have to work very hard to prove to someone that the information you're selling is unique, and so secret that they can only get it from you.

And then, some so-and-so reads your book, or goes to your workshops and starts selling the information themselves.

So the only way you can keep your information unique, and therefore valuable, is to never share it with anyone else. Which kind of defeats the objective of having an information economy!

So what's the answer?

Well people started to talk about the "Knowledge Economy", staffed with "Knowledge Workers"

In the Knowledge Economy, what you sell isn't pure information, its information tempered by experience.

Certainly, overlaying your experience onto information makes it unique. No-one else has exactly the same experiences you have.

But uniqueness--the elusive "USP" you may have heard about--doesn't work anymore. I'll go into that a lot more at the workshop, and what you need to do instead, but let's just say that being Unique is actually a lot harder than the Gurus would have you believe.

In fact, in my Six Figure Blueprint Intensive workshops, I argue that coming up with a USP in the Professional Expert Industry is pretty much impossible. So, if you've been struggling to come up with your niche and your USP, the Six-Figure Blueprint Intensive could be exactly what you need. I'll tell you more about that later.

But I was talking about the knowledge economy.

Knowledge is great, but it doesn't get results. If it did, everyone would be a millionaire, with a perfect relationship, an ideal body, stellar career, achieving all their dreams and aspirations, and the world would be a much happier place. All you'd have to do to be successful would be go out and get some training, put it into practice, and learn from experience.

So why doesn't it work that way?

Part of the reason is that people still don't know what to do with knowledge. Having all the knowledge in the world—all the information and experience—doesn't make someone an expert.

Think about it in your own case. What makes you an expert is that yes, you've got all this information about your field; yes, you've got a lot of experience; but more—much more—than that, you've spent time reflecting on that experience.

It's that reflection that takes knowledge and turns it into wisdom. What's interesting though is what happens with that wisdom, or more specifically what you (as a coach or consultant or trainer) do with that wisdom: you turn it into concrete recommendations and implementation.

People want to be told what to do and how to do it. And if you can do it for them, so much the better.

It's that simple.

We live in an information-overloaded, time-starved, attention-depleted culture. People want quick fixes.

We have to give it to them.

That gets their attention. THEN we can get them to slow down and think about where to go from there. But until you get to that point the conversation is going nowhere.

Here's what I see most professionals doing, and they wonder why they struggle to get clients.

Imagine you have toothache. It's constant. It gnaws away at you. It keeps you awake. It's stopping you from eating and drinking.

So, you go to the dentist. What do you want the dentist to do? You want them to drill and fill, right?

So now imagine that instead your dentist sits you down and starts asking to you about what changes you might be willing to make to your diet. Perhaps cutting down on fizzy drinks might help. How many would you be willing to go down to? What about sweets? …

Would you hear ANY of the conversation?

Would you CARE what the dentist was saying?

No. You just want the pain to stop.

It doesn't mean the conversation the dentist wants to have with you isn't valuable. It's just that in that precise moment it's not the right conversation. In that moment it's value is zero compared to the conversation you want to have (open your mouth, this may hurt a bit…)

Then worse still, they start to ask how you'll feel when the pain is gone. And how much worse does the pain have to get before you do something about it. And you're thinking "I thought I HAD done something about it. That's why I came to you!"

Most of the people who come to you have a pain they want you to take away. And most coaches professionals off into the wrong conversation. Then they wonder why clients go off and find someone else.

A dentist who has a drill and is prepared to use it.

Of course, some people go to the dentist and they're happy to have that conversation. After all, it means they don't have to face up to their fear of the drill.

They may even ask the dentist to just give them advice. So they take the leaflets and they make the changes, and they take a couple of aspirin, but the pain is still there. And all the time the cavity is getting worse.

In fact, it's a pretty poor dentist who lets their clients get away with that if you ask me. It's a dentist who is failing at their most basic responsibility of patient care.

So, clients want knowledge, they want wisdom, but they also want action.

You need to provide the roadmap, get them started and keep them on the path.

The roadmap is what I call your Signature System. How you get them started and keep them on the path is through your Signature Programme.

When you structure your Signature System and your Signature Programme correctly, to achieve the proper objectives, it becomes a high-value offer. In fact it becomes your Mafia Offer (think about it!)

OK. So you need a system, a programme and an offer they can't refuse. What's next?

Well it leads us very neatly into a conversation about conversations.

CLIENTS = CONVERSATIONS

In the Six-Figure Blueprint Intensive I teach 16 principles—I call them Power Principles—which represent new ways of thinking; the ways six- and seven-figure experts think in growing their business.

Two of those Principles are about conversations, so you can tell I hold conversations to be *very* important in growing your business:

1.   Clients = Conversations

2.   Natural Experts join and guide Conversations

Let's look at the first of those.

One of the key things I discovered while building my business was that the quality of the conversations you have will dictate the quality of your business results.

To put it another way "clients = conversations"

Think about it like this.

Most of the professional experts I speak to who are still struggling face one of four problems.

1.   They can't get enough clients

2.   They have enough clients, but they can't charge enough

3. they have enough clients, their fees are good, but they're not the "right" clients

4. they have good clients, paying good money, but they feel like their business is out of control, like it's taking over their life and there aren't enough hours in the day any more

Let's take each of those in turn

Not Enough Clients

If you're not getting enough clients, then ask yourself one simple question. Are you talking to enough people? Are you having enough conversations?

When I started my business, I was excited about the possibilities this new-fangled thing called the Internet was opening up. I sat at home and designed my website. I designed brochures to download, and business cards. I wrote ebooks people would download from my website.

The only thing I didn't do was get out of the door or get on the phone and talk to people.

However much technology can help us build our business (and it can--getting your web presence right is a cornerstone of the Natural Expert system I share in The Six-Figure Blueprint Intensive), there's no substitute for engaging people in conversation.

That conversation can take many forms. You can meet people one-to-one, you can talk to groups, you can

engage with your audience through social media--
whatever it is, make sure you can engage in a TWO-
WAY conversation.

The mistake a lot of marketers make is that they
confuse broadcasting with engagement. Your audience
wants you to engage with them.

So, get out and have more conversations.

Can't Charge Enough

If you're struggling to achieve the fees you want and
deserve, then the conversations you're having don't
create enough value. Another of the Power Principles is
"Money follows value". The fees you can charge
directly reflect the amount of value you're creating for
your clients, and that starts with the value you create in
your conversations.

So, if you want to charge more, have higher-value
conversations.

Not The Right Clients

OK, I shouldn't need to say this by now, but if you're
not getting the right clients, guess what's wrong with
your conversations? That's right: you're not having
conversations with the right people.

If you're a business expert, you need to be talking to
business owners. If you're a relationship expert, talk to
people with relationship issues (and remember that
being in a good relationship and wanting it to stay that

way or even improve is as much an issue as being in a bad relationship or being in no relationship at all!). If you're a parenting expert, go and talk to parents.

The mistake many professionals make is they try to talk to everyone in the hope that their ideal client is lurking somewhere. Focus on having the right conversations with the right people and you'll get the right clients for you. And yes, people know people who know people, but never mistake networking for marketing!

Out Of Control

No, I'm not going to tell you that your conversations are out of control. But I *am* going to tell you that you're not having the conversations you need to.

If your business is out of control then you need to think about boundaries. Are your clients taking up too much time? Or expecting you to be available at unreasonable times? Talk to them about what they can expect from you. And don't be afraid to sack clients who don't want to accept those boundaries.

Are other areas of life encroaching? Then you may need to have a boundaries conversation there too.

And finally, maybe you also need to have a serious conversation with yourself about boundaries.

Now, I said there were two Power Principles concerned with conversations. Let's look at the second.

NATURAL EXPERTS JOIN AND GUIDE CONVERSATIONS

Imagine you're at a party. There are little groups scattered around the room, and the atmosphere is great.

Suddenly a newcomer arrives. They burst through the door and loudly declare "don't worry everyone, I'm here! Now the party can begin! Gather round and let's talk about me."

What would you do? How would you feel? What would happen to the atmosphere at the party?

Worse, imagine it's your party. And a new guest arrives and suggests everyone should head off to the nearest bowling alley.

What would you do?

You'd do everything you could to stop them, right?

Most marketing for the last 100 years has been like one of those two intrusive guests.

Not exactly effective. And definitely not welcome.

Unless your party was *really* boring, in which case you deserve to lose your guests.

So then marketers got smart.

They realised some people might be more receptive than others. So they carved out a niche.

Now I'm pretty sure you've been told you need to find a niche.

You need to target your marketing to a particular group of people, or to solving a particular problem.

And maybe you resisted and fought against it. That's a fear-based response, because professionals worry that if they're not getting clients now, when they're talking to everyone about everything, then surely it'll be even harder if they start ruling people out?

Or maybe you wrestled long and hard to find a niche, you struggled with your fears but overcame them and finally settled on something you felt you could make work. And you reluctantly took down certain pages of your website, retired some of your brochures and case studies, and settled in for the money to start rolling in at last.

After all, that's what the gurus told you would happen.

But for some reason it didn't, or it came in but still too slowly: certainly not "rolling".

What's going on?

Well, to me, having a niche just means you're interrupting the party one group at a time.

It's still not particularly welcome, and it's not guaranteed to be effective.

Which leaves us with a problem. What's the alternative?

Imagine it's you turning up at the party.

You wander round the party and you overhear a few of the groups having conversations that you can contribute to and add value to.

So you join the conversation, adding to what is being said and engaging with the members of the group together and individually.

Later, people come up to you one-to-one. "I was really interested in what you said about X. Can we talk about it more?"

Other groups notice that your group is engaged and enthusiastic, and when you wander to the bar for a drink, someone stops you on the way back and engages you in a new conversation.

Hey, you're popular! You're the life and soul of the party!

How does this play out in the real world?

Back in the 1980s, getting a photocopy in an office environment meant going down to the copy room, where you had a 90% chance of finding a Xerox copier the size of a small car. You'd fill out a job requisition form, leave the form and your original document with the print room staff, and eventually, a day or two later if you were lucky, your job would get processed and you'd get your copies.

That was the way of the world. And there wasn't much of an alternative. If you were typing or writing something yourself you could use carbon paper, and if the document was something pre-done you could use a Gestetner machine, as long as you didn't mind it being purple.

Or you could just write it out again!

Canon wanted to get into the copier market and challenge Xerox's market dominance.

Now they could have taken Xerox on head-to-head ("hey everyone, why don't you leave this party and come with me?").

But it's pretty hard work to take on a dominant player in any market.

Now, while all this was going on, what was happening in businesses? What kinds of conversations were going on at the water cooler?

"Why do I have to walk to the basement to make a copy? Why do I have to wait 2 days for my copies? What use are copies if I can't have them in time for the meeting where I want to discuss them? Why does the print room refuse to make less than 10 copies? Why can't I have my own copier in my office?"

Now Xerox wouldn't have cared about those conversations: big companies were tied into long contracts for paper, ink and maintenance. They could give away copiers and still make money.

But it should have cared.

Because Canon's move was to join the water cooler conversation.

"Yeah, that's a real pain. Wouldn't it be great if you could have a small copier right on your desktop? Wouldn't it be great to be able to copy a single sheet if you needed to? Wouldn't it be great if you could choose where to buy your paper and shop around? And how about if you had a copier that could be fixed by anyone with a brain, rather than having to call an engineer?"

And people welcomed them into the conversation.

So Canon quickly built a business based on desktop copiers. And moved into the copy room not long after that.

In fact, Xerox now has a single-figure market share, and for the last seven years, Canon has been the market leader for copiers.

Apple did the same with the iPod. Other ways of listening to music on the move existed. But people would say "why do I have to carry a suitcase full of cassettes with me every time I go on holiday? If I want an MP3, how can I be sure it's legal? And why do I have to visit 100 websites in order to get the music I want? How can I be sure this random website asking me for my credit card details is legitimate? How do I know what I'm downloading is a music file and not a virus?"

And so they introduced the killer combination of iPod + iTunes.

The iPad was an answer to "why do I have to carry a big laptop around with me? Why can't I have a device that's as easy to use and carry around as my phone, but with a decent screen, so that I can check email and browse the web when I'm on the move?"

So being the Natural Expert in your field is all about understanding what it is that you do best—your natural expertise—who exactly is your client—I call it finding your "Angela")—and then finding out where they are conversing and what conversations they are having.

Then you join that conversation and guide it in the direction that positions you best to help Angela.

MONEY FOLLOWS VALUE

Another of the One of the things I discovered in reflecting on how I grew my coaching and consulting business is that I had unwittingly stumbled on what Jay Abraham--one of the most respected marketers in the world--calls the "Strategy of Pre-eminence".

At the heart of everything I do is the simple principle of creating massive amounts of real value for your audience. That, more than anything else, is the key to creating a tribe around yourself and building a relationship with them.

Traditional marketers say "find people who want what you do or make, get them to pay you and then deliver huge amounts of value so they'll come back."

My business took off when I started to take a very different attitude towards value.

Put very simply, find all the people you want to do business with, and commit to the idea that you're not going to wait for money to change hands before you start to deliver value.

(I suggest you re-read that last paragraph a couple of times, to make sure it really sinks in)

Everyone in your audience is your client, regardless of whether they happen to have paid you yet.

If you go out, find your audience, and contribute, guide, counsel, advise and protect them, the people who value what you are doing the most will come to you eager to do business with you.

Everything I do in business has been based on that simple philosophy since 2005--and "coincidentally" that was the year my income went from almost zero to six figures in a matter of months.

OK in the next chapter I'll ask you a question very few experts ever really consider.

WHO IS YOUR MARKETING FOR?

It's an interesting question isn't it?

The mistake a lot of professional experts make is that their marketing is for them. In other words, it's all about how great their product is, and why you should buy it. So their key measure of success--and therefore their focus--is the sales that come out of the marketing.

Remember, though, that I said Money follows Value, and that your conversations need to create value for your audience. The way to achieve that is to think about what your marketing can achieve for your audience.

You may have heard "talk about benefits, not features. That's why your marketing doesn't work." So you go away, rewrite your website and your brochure, turn all the features ("weekly coaching calls") into benefits ("the programme is structured to hold you accountable and maintain momentum in achieving X"). And still no-one comes. What's wrong now?

Well, when you tell people about benefits, you're still talking about why they should choose you over someone else. But think about why people go searching on the internet, or subscribe to your list. They're looking for solutions. So your marketing needs to help them start to solve the immediate problem.

Think of it this way: when you start to write a marketing message, ask yourself, "how can I help my clients when they read this message, at the same time as I make them aware of me?"

A lot of professional experts are scared to give away "too much"; in particular they don't want to give away the "how". Well, if your audience doesn't get the how from you, they'll only get it from someone else.

Your job is to address the real problem. For most people, "how" isn't the problem. They know what they should do. The challenge is doing it. So tell them what to do and then tell them how you can help them to get it done.

For example, The Six-Figure Blueprint Intensive forces you to step back from all the "stuff" (technical term) that's preventing you from getting down to doing what you need to do. Taking time out in a seminar—especially one that isn't just about a few hundred people listening to rehashes of the same tired old models for two days—gives you space to plan, talk your ideas through with an expert, get feedback from others who are on the same journey, and above all start to implement.

Then we spend pretty much half a day talking about how to get stuff done. The focus is firmly on implementation; how and where to get things

It's not often that we get the time in the "real world" to sit back for two days and work on the business rather than in it (to coin a sadly very overworked phrase, but true nevertheless).

And it's even rarer to get the chance to plan how to get more done while reducing our workload!

If you want to succeed in building your business the fact is you need to create that space, and take it when the opportunity arises.

THE BIGGEST BUSINESS CARD IN THE WORLD

2011 was a great year for me. One of the highlights was writing and publishing my first marketing book for coaches and consultants, "More Clients, More Money, More Fun".

At the Six-Figure Blueprint Intensive, alongside the Power Principles—new ways of thinking—that I share, I also identify nine "Cash Machine" strategies and systems that I have observed in every six- and seven-figure expert business I know.

One of these, and arguably the most important in terms of establishing your position as THE expert in your field, is what I call your "Expert Manifesto"—a book which you can use to position yourself and to generate leads.

Even though society as a whole seems to be leaving books behind, when it comes to choosing our "experts" we still hold authors in awe.

So one of the key things I encourage all my clients to do is to write a book; a physical book, not an ebook (we discuss why in the Six-Figure Blueprint Intensive).

It doesn't have to be War and Peace.

In fact, I see a role for two kinds of books in building your business.

The first is short books or booklets like this one, covering specific aspects of your audience's problem or explaining the big picture of your System. They're great to give away to prospective clients.

The second is longer books that position you as THE expert. It's your opportunity to tell the world not just what you do, but how you do it, and if you can the results that you achieve. These are the ones I consider your true Expert Manifesto.

Imagine this. You're pitching for a piece of work. Your competitor has just come out of the meeting, having left the potential client with a brochure and their business card. You walk in and hand over a copy of your book. Maybe you even offer to sign it for them. Who are they more likely to hire?

Or, a client is looking for advice in your area of expertise. They look on Amazon and find your book listed, with a link to your website. They follow the link. Are they more likely to hire you than someone who just found your name on Google?

Most experts have at least one book inside them that is screaming to get out. The main challenges that hold them back, however, are

1. getting it written

2. getting it published

I could write a whole book about those challenges, so I can't do them justice in a short book like this.

The biggest problem is that by focusing down on very specific clients and their problems—in using your book to join a conversation—you become totally unappealing to traditional publishers.

Mainstream publishers are looking for books with mass appeal, not highly targeted books with limited appeal outside a tightly defined audience.

That leaves the expert looking at options such as self-publishing and print-on-demand.

A large part of the second day of my Six-Figure Blueprint Intensive is devoted to writing and publishing your book, but at the end of the day the reality is that producing a professional looking book—whatever other people might tell you—takes time, money and professional support.

For that reason my Protégé mentoring programs include support to get your book planned, written, edited, typeset, published and launched onto the global stage.

And since the point I make is that you should get support from experts, I created a strategic alliance with the UK's leading writers' coach and a professional publishing company.

That way, my clients have access to the best possible support in getting their books out into the market as quickly as possible.

YOUR "BIG BACK END"

Earlier I discussed why the traditional sales funnel doesn't work. Which leaves a question hanging in the air: "do I need products at all then?"

After all, if you're selling people straight into a £7,000 or more programme, and there's no sales funnel as we normally understand it, surely products don't matter?

Well yes, and no. the good news is, I can show you how to build a highly profitable, but still "leveraged" coaching business without having to create products. But still suggest you do create products.

It's just I don't think you should waste your time creating £17 CDs.

There are 4 kinds of product in the Natural Expert system.

1. "Components" are integral elements of your Signature Programme. For example, the programme might include access to a webinar series, a membership site, or perhaps a home study kit that supports the content you are teaching directly. Components increase the perceived value of the programme, so they need to be high-end products!

2. "Bonuses" are rewards for some optional aspect of the buying process (such as acting before a deadline). Again, you want your

bonuses to be high value (so that they are persuasive) not a cheap ebook.

Another of the Cash Machines in the Natural Expert System is having a back-end. However, unlike a "traditional" guru-model back end, the purpose is primarily to maintain engagement with members of your tribe until they're ready to work with you on a high-end program and with past clients until they're ready to make the next step. This gives us the remaining two types of product:

3. "Accelerators": these get people in your community to come to your Signature Seminar.

4. "Retainers": these are what you give people who have been through your programme as a way of staying in your Tribe.

But here's the key point. In the Guru model, you pretty much don't have a business until you build your sales funnel and your back-end. In the Natural Expert System, these products are a nice-to-have. You can start building a business, and quite feasibly take it to six-figures, without products.

Each of the four uses of products requires different characteristics, however there is one key characteristic shared by all of them: you need to create a product that is used from start to finish. If the user never gets to the end of the product they aren't going to be satisfied. They'll claim against your guarantees, and they're unlikely to buy anything else from you. Across the coaching and consulting industry, 80% of products are abandoned less than 20% of the way through. And it has nothing to do with the investment required: I personally have a $3,000 product I bought from a well-known "guru" in 2008 that I never got past CD 3 and DVD 1 of!

So what's the secret? It's about how you structure the product, how you present it, and how you assemble the content. Again, there's more to tell you than I can do justice to in this book, so if you can't make it to a Six-Figure Blueprint Intensive, just bear in mind that you need to make sure your products:

a) Meet the objectives for the type of product you're creating

b) Achieve the educational and value-creation objectives you've set for that product, and

c) Are designed from the ground up to make sure the buyer makes it all the way through

So, now that we have our back end in place, let's see what we can do about getting people buying from you.

Coach Don't Sell

Most coaches hate to sell. And you can tell, because as soon as they need to sell, they go into a completely different way of acting and speaking. You can tell they're not comfortable.

And that's fine, because most people hate being sold to. The moment you start to sell, they put up what I call the "bull" filter (actually, live I use a slightly longer name, but I'm sure you get the picture).

If you switch into sales mode suddenly, it doesn't matter how much rapport you had before, you're back to square one, and your audience is now in a bad mood.

So how would it be if you never had to sell again if you didn't want to?

The good thing is that while people hate being sold to, they do love to buy.

So you have to make them want to buy.

And the way to do that is to educate them to want what you are offering.

There are all sorts of ways to do this. Stories are one great way to teach and sell at the same time, especially your own story, which is why I devote time with my clients to teaching them how to structure, write and tell their personal Expert Story so that it becomes a key tool for pre-selling clients before they've even met you, rather than some interesting content for your online profiles!

Stories are also a great way of overcoming people's fears and prejudices.

Which brings me to a key point about your conversations, and that is to position yourself as the "antidote" to people's fears and prejudices about your industry.

That really does give you a unique position, and one that naturally draws people to you.

You see, whatever you do, people will have preconceptions about it. As soon as you say "I'm an X", they stop listening to you and start an internal conversation that goes something like: "oh no, not another X. They're the people who make you…, and they're so…, and I don't like the way they…" and so on and so forth.

At that point you've lost them.

It's one of the reasons I never describe myself as a "coach" (or consultant for that matter) to general business audiences. I talk about the kinds of clients I've worked with. I talk about their problems. And I talk about results. I get them to connect to what it would be like to be rid of their biggest problem.

When I'm making a sales presentation I don't talk about coaching. Because no-one cares about coaching, except coaches. I don't talk about my coaching certifications and accreditations, because the only people who care about those are coaches. And I don't talk about my coaching style because the only people who care about that are… well I'm sure you can finish that sentence ;-)

Of course, in order to address your audience's fears and prejudices you need to know your audience really well. And that means treating them as something much more than just a "niche".

That's why a major section of The Six-Figure Blueprint Intensive is devoted to exactly that: not just knowing your niche, but understanding your audience at a deep level and using that to have much deeper and value-rich conversations with them.

You Don't Have To Do It Alone

One lesson I learned very early on in growing my business was that you don't have to do it alone—whatever your "it" happens to be.

Since I turned my business around in 2005, one of the biggest influences on my success has been the strength of the partnerships I have cultivated.

There's something very coach-like about the idea of a joint venture.

In a joint venture, you find another business that serves the same clients as you, but provides a complementary service (i.e. that does not compete with your own services).

Back in 2005, JVs were one of the key ways that I built my business. My first JV was a good learning opportunity (I made $0 from it), but my third brought me more than £250k/$400k over a period of a three years.

The difference? When I set up my first JV I came at it with the wrong mindset, and I was unprepared for the follow-up.

I'd expected a stream of leads would be attracted by my partner's reputation, and the leads generated would magically turn into clients.

It just doesn't work that way.

By the time of my third JV I had a strong offer in place, and the JV was with someone who operated in a market in which I had a strong track record, proven results and credibility.

That JV partner's list was highly targeted, very relevant to the offer I was making and had a track record of buying.

And when I spoke to the prospects that came through that partner I was able to connect to them through my own experience. I spoke their language, I showed I understood their problems, and I demonstrated knowledge of the culture in that market.

I'd found someone who had access to a lot of my "Angelas" (I'll explain who Angela is in the workshop!), and my Angelas were who they were because I had a strong affinity with them.

And the JV partner got HUGE amounts of value from the partnership.

Most importantly, though, we both approached the venture strategically: it was a long term relationship for both of us.

Between them, those factors make up the secret to finding a good JV relationship.

Now, a lot of coaches tell me that they have trouble finding JV partnerships.

The biggest problem is that they come at the potential partnership with a mindset of "how can I get this person to help me build my business".

Here's the shocker.

People are too busy building their own business to help you build yours.

I'll say it again.

People are too busy building their own business to help you build yours

So you have to take a different approach.

You have to ask yourself "how can I build my business by helping this person to build theirs".

In fact, turn that on its head.

"How can building this person's business grow mine?"

You see, that first question has many answers.

Be creative about how you can help them.

And when you've answered that—and only when you've answered that—start to think about how you can get benefit from that situation too.

ENGAGING YOUR TRIBE

One of the keys to building a great business, and getting people to engage with you on high-end coaching programmes, is to deliver a great experience, and to engage with people throughout the process, not just as part of the transaction.

One great way of getting people to engage is through participation, and the good news is that thanks to social media it's never been easier--or cheaper--to get people to participate.

Amazon is a great example of driving participation with very little input from the business itself: people review items, give feedback on other people's reviews ("was this review helpful?"), create and share wishlists, and a myriad of other "social" features that turn a simple ecommerce site into a virtual community.

The most popular shows on TV are often the ones where viewers can vote, and so control the outcome: Strictly Come Dancing, X Factor, Big Brother...

The free webinar platform MeetingBurner.com (well worth trying out by the way) has brought a whole new level of engagement to webinars by adding a live feedback feature: participants can move an on-screen slider to let the speaker know if what they're saying is hot or not. I LOVE it!!!

At a minimum you should encourage people to engage with you on social media. For example, you can interact with me on

- Facebook:
  http://www.facebook.com/6FigureBlueprint

- My blog: http://robcuesta.typepad.com/

- YouTube: www.youtube.com/robcuesta

- Twitter: www.twitter.com/robcuesta

- LinkedIn:
  http://uk.linkedin.com/in/robcuesta

- and many other places online.

It's all about creating those conversations I was talking about earlier in this book.

The ultimate engagement, of course, is face-to-face, which is why I look forward to engaging with you live and in person at one of my Six-Figure Blueprint Intensives!

THE SIX-FIGURE BLUEPRINT INTENSIVE

Hopefully by now you've got an idea of the kind of things I share at the Six-Figure Blueprint Intensive.

Every time I talk about the workshop to a professional expert, they tell me they're sick of going to workshops where they sit in a crowd of 300 and get told all of these things they "should" be doing, but there's absolutely no guidance on what the priorities are, what order things need to get done in, and even more importantly HOW to do everything that needs to be done and still have time to deliver to their clients.

So I designed The Six-Figure Blueprint Intensive to be the exact opposite of the workshops you're used to seeing.

Saturday morning I show you why the traditional approach to building a coaching business--the way everyone else tells you to do it--is a waste of time; and how I built a six-figure coaching and consulting business while breaking every rule in the book.

I share the only 9 systems you have to implement in your business to achieve the lifestyle and financial success that accompanies being a true expert in your field and having the impact in the world you aspire to.

That's it.

With those 9 systems you have everything you need. So we spend the rest of the two days learning how to implement each of them.

Saturday afternoon we look at how you can reinforce in the minds of your audience that you are THE expert at what you do, and there's no point them talking to (or hiring) anyone else.

Then we look at exactly what your online presence needs to look like, even down to what pages you need on your website, what needs to be on those pages, and what you should be doing, where, in social media.

On Sunday morning I tell you about exciting developments like my alliance with a publishing house and the UK's leading book coach, which means my clients can write their books quickly and get them professionally published and onto bookshelves *across the world*.

Then we look at the biggest lie in marketing, and I relieve you of the burden of building a huge list (and tell you what you need to do instead).

Having given you all of this "stuff" to do, I talk to you (Sunday afternoon) about how to get it done AND create the space to focus on your natural strengths and your natural expertise.

And then finally, I put it together for you step by step, month by month, into a blueprint for success.

Now, does that sound like other workshops you've been to? If it does then I haven't done justice to what the weekend is about.

And because I know you're probably a little sceptical after all the workshops you've been to where you didn't get anything new, I have a guarantee that says you can stay until the end and if you didn't learn anything new I'll refund your investment. No questions asked.

I can't make the offer any easier to accept than that!

And to finish, I thought I'd share part of a conversation I had last night with a coach.

She asked me what the workshop was about, and after 30 seconds she said "I need to be there!"

What had I said to her?

Simple, I told her that in 3 months last year I sold £124,000 of high-end coaching and training programmes to people who hadn't had to go through a long sales funnel of low cost products.

In fact, they'd never even heard of me before that point.

And in the Six-Figure Blueprint Intensive I share what I learned doing that.

(And bear in mind all of that was on top of the corporate coaching and training work I sold which takes me travelling across the globe as the trusted expert to some of the world's largest companies).

So, the question you need to ask yourself is "would I like to be able to sell people straight into high-end coaching programmes (and by 'high-end' I mean programmes at £7,500, £15,000 or even more) from cold? Do I want to know how to create 'big pay days' easily, and earn more in a weekend than most coaches make in a whole year?"

That's the power of positioning yourself as the Natural Expert in your field.

If that sounds interesting, then book your place at www.RobCuesta.com/6figureblueprint.

That's it. I'm keeping it short and sweet because you know by now if the weekend is right for you.

I'd love to catch up with you at a Six-Figure Blueprint Intensive, and find out how you're getting on, but above all I'd love to share my knowledge, my expertise and my reflections on the last 10 years of running my business.

All the best, and here's to a fantastic future as the Natural Expert in your field!!

Rob Cuesta
March 2012

WHAT PEOPLE SAY

"I Unearthed £20,000 of Additional Revenue I'd Previously Overlooked"

Suddenly I could see a way forward and the pieces of the jigsaw began to fall slowly into place; a clear step by step detailed action plan was shaped and formed, and I know I can realistically achieve the targets set. I also learned huge amounts about myself, but the icing on the cake was unearthing a potential £20,000 of additional revenue I'd previously overlooked.

Allison Marlowe

Hampshire Winning Women, Fareham

"I Had 35% More Sales From My Current Business In The Last 6 Months"

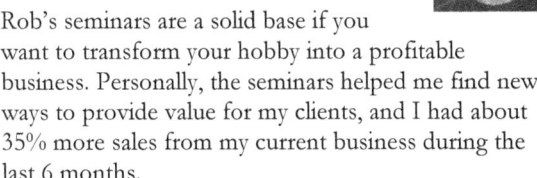

Rob's seminars are a solid base if you want to transform your hobby into a profitable business. Personally, the seminars helped me find new ways to provide value for my clients, and I had about 35% more sales from my current business during the last 6 months.

Tadas Pakalnis

Relationship Expert, London

"In Just Under 6 Months The Results Have Been Phenomenal"

In just under 6 months the results have been phenomenal: I have written and printed my first book, which is getting great reviews, and I've turned my coaching into a programme that is much easier to pitch.

Alain Balanche-Jacquet

The Success Mindset Coach, Birmingham

"I Can Spend More Time Coaching and Earning Money"

Rob Cuesta has provided me with a clear, logical and effective blueprint on how to cut through all the confusing noise around marketing, both on-line and off-line.

I have now been able to create a professional marketing strategy and put it on automatic so that rather than spend time struggling to find clients, I can spend more time coaching and earning money.

George Pirintzi

Relationship Coach, London

"I can market myself in a way that honours my deepest values"

I came to the workshop wondering if I would learn anything. What I learned is that I can market myself in a way that honours my deepest values: "marketing" is neither good nor bad – it is how you use it that matters, and Rob showed me many ways to use it with positive intent.

Chris de Castell
Integrated Light, Toronto

"Rob Clarified The Steps To Bring My Business To The Next Level"

Rob's expertise and models not only clarified the steps necessary to bring my business to the next level but it also helped clarify my vision and purpose.

His humour, passion, integrity and knowledge shine through with every word.

I highly recommend Rob to anyone looking to increase value in their business.

Len Benoit
NLP Centres Canada, Toronto

MORE TESTIMONIALS AT WWW.ROBCUESTA.COM/TESTIMONIALS

WORKING WITH ROB CUESTA

To find out more about how you can work with Rob Cuesta more closely:

- visit www.RobCuesta.com/workwithus or

- email enquiries@robcuesta.com

If you'd like to a more in depth discussion then call our international offices on

- +44 207 193 2181 (UK/Europe) or

- +1 202 657 5687 (USA/Canada/rest of the world)

READER OFFER

I trust that you have found the information in this booklet not just interesting, but useful, valuable and above all practical.

I hope that it is the start of a relationship that will grow and deepen, and I'd like to help that process on its way.

As part of that, I have a very special offer to make to you.

In this short booklet I have only had space to share just a little of what I know with you. But I'd like to share more.

As a reader of this book I'd like to offer you an 80% discount against the advertised enrolment fee for The Six-Figure Blueprint Intensive.

For forthcoming dates and venues, and to reserve your place visit:

www.robcuesta.com/6figureblueprint

To claim your discounted rate, enter the promotion code **secretbook** when ordering your ticket(s).